DON'T WASTE THE PAIN

DON'T WASTE THE PAIN

When Pain Meets Purpose

Maurice Elston

DEDICATION

To my twin daughters, Reese and Reagan—my greatest inspirations. You are the reason I knew something had to change, the force that pushed me toward growth, and the light that keeps me moving forward. This book exists because of you.

To Leah "Butta" Nicole—when this book was nothing more than an idea in my heart, you spoke life into me. Your unwavering love, encouragement, and belief in me pushed me beyond my limits. I could not have done this without you.

To my parents—THANK YOU! You always told me I could be anything I put my mind to, and because of you, I have finally found my purpose.

To my brother, my right hand—thank you for making sure I never gave up. Look at me now, bro—a published author.

Last, but never least, to my Lord and Savior, Jesus Christ—you gave me the words to write and the ability to bring them to life. I love you, Lord, and I pray this book reaches exactly who You intend for it to reach

TABLE OF CONTENTS

PREFACE

This book was birthed from pain and matured through healing. It is the result of a journey—one filled with heartbreak, loss, self-doubt, and redemption. I have endured many wounds in life—some inflicted by others, and many that I placed upon myself. For years, I wrestled with the weight of my experiences, questioning why pain had been such a constant companion. I often found myself wondering how a loving God could allow His people to suffer. Was there a purpose to all this suffering, or was it an unavoidable part of life?

Like many, I sought answers. I tried to outrun pain, to numb it, to deny its existence. But pain is persistent. It does not disappear when ignored—it demands to be felt, to be acknowledged, to be understood. It wasn't until I reached my lowest moments, standing on the edge of despair, that I allowed myself to lean into the very thing spent so long avoiding. In the darkness, I began to see the light. In the struggle, I found strength. And in the pain, I discovered purpose.

This book is a labor of love, a guide for anyone who ever questioned the reason behind their suffering. It is my deepest desire to help others navigate their own pain—not to endure it, but to embrace it, to learn from it, and to allow it to shape them into something stronger, wiser, and more whole. Pain is not a cruel affliction; it is also a teacher. If we are willing to listen, it can reveal lessons that will transform us in ways we never imagined.

I do not claim to have all the answers, but I do know this—pain, when embraced with an open heart, can be one of the most powerful forces of growth. It has the ability to break us, yes, but also to rebuild us into something greater than before. My hope is that within these pages, you will find comfort, understanding, and the encouragement to keep going, when the road feels impossible.
You are not alone. And your pain is not in vain.

Let's embark on this journey together.

INTRODUCTION

Pain is one thing that is inevitable in every person's life. It's unrelenting, consistent reminder that we are all human—nowhere close to being invincible. No matter where you grew up, your social status, the amount of money in your bank account, your ethnicity, or your religious beliefs, pain is a universal experience. None of us can escape it. And yet, though pain is unavoidable, it often catches us off guard, shaking the foundation of everything we thought we knew about ourselves and the world.

In those moments, when pain is overwhelming, have you ever stopped to ask: Why do I have to suffer? What is the purpose of this pain? How long will this last? We've all wrestled with these burning questions in one form or another. Pain demands answers. It demands explanations. It forces us to confront truths we'd often rather ignore.

For years, I tried to make sense of the pain I experienced. Some of it came into my life without warning or permission—caused by the choices and actions of others. Other times, I had no one to blame but myself. The truth is, some of the deepest wounds I've endured were self-inflicted, brought on by my own bad decisions, patterns, and habits.

But no matter where the pain came from, the questions were the same. Why me? Why now? And for a long time, I didn't have answers.

One season of pain I'll never forget was a true turning point in my life—one that still shapes me today. One night, driving alone, I was hit by a storm of emotions I didn't yet know how to navigate. My wife at the time had told me she was leaving. I didn't blame her. In fact, I knew I had played a major role in pushing her to that point. It wasn't sudden; it was the result of things I did—or failed to do—over time. Looking back, I can say she needed to leave. But knowing that didn't make the moment any less excruciating.

I remember the sinking feeling of knowing that everything I worked to build—my marriage, my family, my sense of stability—was falling apart right in front of me. I was overwhelmed with guilt, anger, and shame. I was losing everything: her, myself, and the life I thought I would always have.

That night, as I drove in silence, I turned to God. I didn't have any eloquent prayers or profound words. It was a raw, desperate plea for clarity. I asked, What now? How am I supposed to move forward from here?

And in that quiet, broken moment, God impress these words on my heart: Don't waste the pain.

At first, I didn't understand. I sat with those words for days, turning them over in my mind. Don't waste the pain. What does that mean? How do you waste pain? Wasn't it something to endure until it passed?

Over the weeks and months that followed, I began to realize what those words meant. Pain isn't something we survive—it's something we can learn from. It's not a storm we wait out—it's a teacher that can show us who we really are, what we're capable of, and what matters.

But here's the thing: not everyone learns those lessons. Some people waste their pain. They push it down, numb it, or avoid it altogether. And when they do, they miss the chance to grow. They miss the chance to let pain shape them into wiser, stronger, and more compassionate individuals.

I've learned that wasting pain means refusing to engage with it. It means running from it, pretending it isn't there, or ignoring the lessons it's trying to teach us. And I've also learned that not wasting pain—leaning into it, sitting with it, and allowing it to change us—is one of the most courageous things we can do.

This book, Don't Waste the Pain, is about learning how to navigate the painful seasons of life with intention. It's about finding purpose right in the middle of pain, when the path forward feels unclear. It's about choosing to grow, no matter how deep the hurt or how long the road to healing.

Pain doesn't discriminate. It will touch every life at some point—yours, mine, everyone's. But what you do with your pain is what sets you apart. Will you let it harden you, or will you let it refine you? Will you let it make you bitter, or will you let it make you better?

In the pages ahead, we'll explore the lessons that pain offered. Together, we'll uncover how pain can:
- Build resilience by showing us the depths of our strength.
- Deepen empathy by connecting us to the struggles of others.
- Reveal the need for self-awareness and reflection in our lives.
- Highlight the value of joy and peace, so we learn to treasure those moments when they come.
- Teach us patience and acceptance as we wait for healing to come.
- Show us the importance of boundaries and self-care, so we can protect ourselves and grow.
- Remind us of life's temporary nature, encouraging us to stay present and hopeful, in the hardest moments.

This isn't about glorifying pain or pretending it's easy. Pain is hard. It's messy, uncomfortable, and sometimes lonely. But it doesn't have to be wasted.

No matter what kind of pain you're facing—whether it's heartbreak, loss, failure, betrayal, or regret—this book is for you. It's for the person who is stuck in their suffering and wonders if they'll ever make it to the other side. It's for anyone who's asked, Why me? and longs to find purpose in the mess of it all.

Pain is inevitable, but wasting it is not. It can break you, or it can build you. My hope is that this book will help you choose the latter. Let's walk through this together, one step at a time. And let's make the decision today: **We won't waste the pain.**

CHAPTER 1

PAIN IS INEVITABLE,
BUT GROWTH IS OPTIONAL

Life doesn't seek your permission to hurt you. It strikes when it pleases—unexpected, unrelenting, and unapologetic. Pain spares no one; it has no regard for who you are, what you've built, or how you've planned. It storms in, indifferent to your dreams or progress, leaving you with one choice: how you will respond. The real question isn't if pain will come—it's when. And when it does, will you let it consume you, or will you rise and transform it into something greater? What will you do with it?

I've wrestled with that question, and let me tell you, the answer doesn't come easy. My moment of reckoning came when I walked into my empty house for the first time after my ex-wife moved out. The kids were with my mom for the night, and the silence hit me like a freight train. Furniture was missing, closets bare where her clothes used to be, and it all felt like a hollow echo of the life I thought I built. The tears came—not tears of loss, but tears of shame. Tears for the man I thought I was supposed to be but wasn't.

At the time, I was an elder in my church, a leader people looked to for strength and wisdom. I had my own Christian record label, preached at countless churches, and performed on stages that left crowds clapping. From the outside, I had it all together. But inside, I was crumbling. On stage, with hundreds watching, the hollowness gnawing at me. A voice whispered, "What's the point of all this if you're still broken?" But I buried that voice under applause and success.

"You doing okay, man?" a friend asked one day after preaching at his church, his concern cutting through the mask I wore.

"Yeah, I'm tired," I lied, forcing a smile. Admitting the truth felt like surrender.

The truth was, I made success my identity. The clapping crowds, the adoring messages, the leadership roles—they were all distractions I clung to because they were easier than facing myself. I craved validation more than I craved healing. I used other people's admiration to numb my own inadequacies. But at night, when the world was quiet and I was left alone with my thoughts, it all crumbled away, leaving nothing but the truth of my brokenness.

I was terrified of what I might find if I dug deeper. What if I was never meant to be the man everyone believed I was? What if I was nothing without the accolades and admiration? That fear paralyzed me. Instead of confronting it, I drowned it in busyness and the noise of a packed schedule. If I stayed busy, I wouldn't have to feel anything at all.

There's pain when life happens to you, but a deeper, darker kind of pain when you know you're the one who lit the match. I been so blinded by success and the applause of others that I'd convinced myself I was untouchable. But that illusion was shattered.

Once again, I heard the words, clear as day: "Don't waste this pain." I ignored it. I thought I could keep moving, keep smiling in public, keep pretending. Pride wouldn't let me admit how broken I really was. But every night, when the world quieted down, the pain screamed louder than ever. My daughters, who were two years old at the time, were my only anchor. When I had them, I tried to be present, but they sensed something was off. Their little eyes said, "Daddy, are you okay?"

I wasn't!

I was broken but didn't know it. I was fighting things inside that I didn't even know existed. How do you fight when you don't even know what you are fighting? It's like swinging in the dark— exhausting, aimless, and leaving you more bruised than before.

Therapy helped me start to unravel the mess inside, but I didn't understand how to process anything. To numb the pain, I turned to old habits I'd left behind. The bottle became my companion. I started drinking—not enough to lose control, but enough to take the edge off. I picked up smoking weed again, so I could sleep at night. One night, as I sat on the couch, drink in hand, my phone lit up with a text. "Bro, you good? Haven't seen you around." It was a friend trying to reach me through the haze I'd built around myself. "I'm fine," I typed back. "I needed some space." But the truth was, I didn't want anyone to see the wreckage I become.

I started withdrawing from everyone. Friends. Family. Church. I stopped doing music, I stepped down abrutly from leadership at my church and secluded myself. I couldn't bear anyones well-meaning advice or their questions about my well-being. "How are you holding up?" they'd ask, with eyes filled with concern. I hated that question because I didn't have an answer that felt true. Or maybe I didn't want to admit how lost I was.

I spent hours reflecting on how I got to that place. There were countless missed signs, moments where I chose pride over honesty, applause over authenticity. I had convinced myself that being strong meant never showing weakness. But in reality, the strongest thing I could have done was admit that I wasn't okay.

"This can't be my life," I whispered to the night. "I was supposed to be more than this. So why can't I pull myself out of this hole?" I wanted to blame the world for what happened, but deep down, I knew it was me I couldn't forgive.

No matter what I tried, the pain kept growing. It wasn't going anywhere.

Over the years, I've come to understand that pain is a doorway. It's an invitation to step into a deeper, fuller version of yourself. But you have to walk through it. No one can do it for you. You have to face the fear, the shame, the guilt, and let it teach you. And when you do, you'll discover that the pain you thought would destroy you was actually the thing that saved you.

The thing about pain is that it demands to be felt. You can run from it, numb it, suppress it—but it will wait for you. It will follow you into every relationship, every achievement, every quiet moment. It will whisper in your ear when you least expect it, reminding you of the unresolved wounds you refused to face. And if you're not careful, unprocessed pain will harden you, making you bitter, defensive, and afraid of love and connection.

But here's the other truth: pain can also shape you into something extraordinary. If you let it, pain will teach you resilience. It will carve out a deeper well of compassion within you. It will show you what matters and strip away everything that doesn't. It will break you open so that you can be rebuilt—stronger, wiser, and more whole than before.

So, I'll ask you again: What are you doing with your pain? Have you been wasting it? Have you let it stop you from becoming the person you were meant to be? Or will you choose today to do something different?

Pain is inevitable. Growth is optional. The choice is yours.

Take Action:Today, make a decision. Don't just acknowledge your pain—confront it. Journal about what you're feeling, talk to someone you trust, or take that first step toward healing through therapy, prayer, or meditation. Whatever it is, start now. Your growth begins with one brave choice. Are you willing to make it?

CHAPTER 2

THE WAKE-UP CALL:
FACING THE TRUTH ABOUT PAIN

Pain is our body's way of telling us that something is wrong. Emotional pain works the same way as physical pain because it activates the same areas in the brain—the anterior cingulate cortex and the anterior insula. That's why heartbreak can feel like a "broken heart" or betrayal can feel like a "gut punch." These brain regions help us process pain, both physically and emotionally, ensuring that we not only feel it but also respond to it.

The problem is that most of us ignore what pain is trying to tell us. Instead of facing it, we try to deny, avoid, or numb it. But pain, when ignored, doesn't disappear. It lingers beneath the surface, waiting to be acknowledged. And the longer it goes unaddressed, the more it festers, seeping into other areas of our lives, quietly molding our behaviors, our choices, and our sense of identity.

Running from Pain: The Illusion of Escape

I have done all three—denying, avoiding, and numbing. My pride wouldn't allow me to admit when I was hurting, especially in front of other people. I became an expert at wearing a mask, convincing the world—and sometimes myself—that I was perfectly fine.
"Hey, man, you good?" a friend would ask."I'm managing," I'd say, my voice steady but hollow, hoping they'd drop the subject before my carefully built facade crumbled. Sometimes, the words felt more like a desperate plea than a confident assurance.

The truth was, I was terrified of admitting that I was struggling. I buried myself in work, overloaded my schedule, and surrounded myself with people to avoid being alone with my thoughts. But the busy days and sleepless nights couldn't silence the ache that echoed beneath the surface.

Distractions became my lifeline. I told myself that as long as I kept moving, I wouldn't have to feel the weight of my own reality. Yet, deep down, I knew these temporary escapes were nothing more than flimsy barriers against a flood that would eventually break through.

There's a saying that you can't conquer what you don't confront. Avoiding pain doesn't make it hurt any less; it pushes it further down the road—until one day, you reach a dead end where you have no choice but to face it.

The Dead End: When Avoidance No Longer Works

At that dead end, I turned to things that would numb the pain. I drank more, smoked to sleep, and sought shallow connections. I convinced myself I was having fun, but deep down, I was using substances and people to numb what I didn't want to feel.

"You keep doing the same thing over and over, expecting something to change," I whispered to myself one night, my own voice heavy with resignation. The truth was, I had grown tired of my own games. But admitting that meant taking a hard look at myself—and that was something I wasn't ready to do.

One night, staring at my own reflection with bloodshot eyes, I mumbled, "Why do you do this to yourself?" The next morning, the emptiness returned. I realized that my attempts to escape weren't just hurting me—they were hurting others, too.

Facing Pain: The First Step Toward Healing

It's not that drinking, smoking, or sex are wrong. But when they become tools to escape reality, they become crutches. And crutches are meant to be temporary aids, not permanent solutions.

If you want to heal, you have to stop running. You have to lean into the discomfort and ask: What is this pain trying to teach me? What am I supposed to learn from this?

Practical Strategies for Facing and Processing Pain

- Mindful Journaling: Write down your thoughts and emotions without filtering them. This helps bring unconscious feelings to the surface, making them easier to process.
- Grounding Exercises: When overwhelmed, engage your senses. Identify five things you can see, four you can touch, three you can hear, two you can smell, and one you can taste to reconnect with the present moment.
- Develop a Support Network: Share your journey with trusted friends, family members, or therapists. Genuine connection eases the healing process.
- Practice Self-Compassion: Replace self-criticism with kindness. Healing takes time, and setbacks are part of the process.
- Therapeutic Techniques: Engage in therapies like Cognitive Behavioral Therapy (CBT) or Acceptance and Commitment Therapy (ACT) to reframe negative thoughts and embrace discomfort as part of growth.
- Physical Movement: Exercise, yoga, or walking can help process emotions and release built-up tension.
- Set Boundaries: Protect your mental space by setting healthy boundaries with people and environments that trigger or worsen your pain.
- Reflection Exercises: At the end of each day, ask yourself: "What did I learn from my pain today? How did I respond to it? What will I do differently tomorrow?"

Reflection Prompts:

- What unresolved pain am I carrying?
- What coping mechanisms am I using to avoid facing it?
- What practical steps can I take today to start processing and healing?

Pain is sending you a signal. It's time to acknowledge it, learn from it, and unleash a strength in you that you didn't know you had. The choice is yours: Keep running, or face what has been chasing you all along.

CHAPTER 3

RESILIENCE: DISCOVERING STRENGTH, YOU DIDN'T KNOW YOU HAD

Pain has a way of pushing us to our absolute limits. It drags us to dark, lonely places where hope feels distant and survival seems impossible. But often, it's in these desperate moments—when we feel like we're at our breaking point—that we discover something unexpected: Strength.

Not the kind of strength built from comfort or ease, but the type that's forged in the fire of suffering. True resilience isn't born from success; it's born from struggle. It's the unexplainable force that keeps you standing when everything else is trying to knock you down.

Every one of us has faced pain so deep it feels impossible to overcome. The kind of pain that steals your breath and makes you wonder if you'll ever find joy again. It's the heartbreak of betrayal, the weight of grief, the sting of failure. Pain leaves its mark on all of us, but the difference between staying broken and becoming stronger lies in how we choose to respond.

- How does a parent survive the unbearable grief of losing a child?
- How does someone get up every morning after losing the love of their life?
- How does an athlete find the will to keep going after being told they'll never play again?

Pain of this magnitude makes us question everything—our purpose, our future, and even our identity. It leaves us standing at a crossroads, staring at two paths: One of defeat and one of resilience.

What Is Resilience?

People often talk about resilience as if it's something you're either born with or you're not. But resilience isn't a natural gift; it's something that must be built, strengthened, and chosen over and over again.

Resilience isn't just about enduring pain. It's about adapting to it, growing from it, and using it to become stronger. It's not simply "bouncing back"—it's learning to bounce forward. Resilience is about using pain as fuel for growth, not letting it consume you.

Resilience is the ability to recover, adapt, and grow stronger in the face of adversity. It's about refusing to let hardship define you. It's the emotional strength and mental flexibility to keep moving forward, even when life feels like it's crumbling.

But here's the truth: Resilience doesn't just happen. It doesn't magically appear one day and make life easier. It's a choice you have to make, over and over again.
It's the moment you decide: I won't let this be the end of me.

A Story of Resilience

Let's look at a man we'll call Jordan.

Jordan spent years working toward his dream of becoming a firefighter. He trained relentlessly, passed all the exams, and finally got accepted into the academy. His entire future was in front of him.

Then, one day, everything changed.

During a routine training exercise, Jordan suffered a severe knee injury. The doctors told him he might never regain full strength. They said his dream of becoming a firefighter might be over before it even truly began.

At first, he was devastated. He spiraled into self-doubt, questioning everything he had worked for. Why me? Why now? After everything

I've sacrificed, how could this happen?

But after the initial shock, Jordan made a choice. He wasn't going to let his injury define him.

Rehabilitation was brutal. The pain was unbearable at times, and progress felt agonizingly slow. There were moments when doubt crept in and whispered, Maybe you should just give up.

But Jordan refused.

He leaned on his support system—his family, his friends, his physical therapist. He surrounded himself with people who reminded him that setbacks weren't permanent, that this wasn't the end of his story.

Months later, Jordan wasn't just walking again—he was training harder than ever. His body had changed, but so had his mind. Through his struggle, he developed patience, perseverance, and a resilience he never knew he had.

When he finally returned to the academy, he wasn't just ready. He was stronger. Not just physically, but mentally and emotionally. Jordan's story teaches us something powerful: Setbacks don't define us. Our response to them does.

Three Lessons on Building Resilience

Pain will come. But how we respond determines whether we grow or stay stuck. Here are three essential lessons to help you build resilience:

1. Setbacks Are Temporary, but Growth Is Permanent
- Pain may slow you down, but it doesn't have to stop you.
- Challenges are not dead ends; they're detours leading you to something greater.
- Hard times don't last forever, but the strength you build in them does.

2. Progress Isn't Always Linear
- Healing takes time. Some days you'll move forward, and other days you'll feel like you're slipping back.
- Don't mistake slow progress for failure. Resilience means moving forward, even when progress feels invisible.
- Every small victory strengthens your ability to face the next challenge.

3. Support Systems Matter
- You don't have to do this alone. Resilient people lean on others.
- There's no weakness in asking for help; real strength is knowing when you need support.
- Surround yourself with people who can remind you of your strength when you forget.

The Truth About Resilience

Pain has a way of stripping us down to our rawest form, forcing us to face who we are when everything else falls apart. It challenges us to confront our weaknesses, our fears, and our deepest wounds. But in that breaking, we are given a choice—to remain shattered or to rebuild.

Resilience is not about avoiding pain. It's about letting it refine you. It's about allowing pain to carve out strength where there was once weakness, to awaken something within you that comfort never could.

If you are in pain right now, remember this: Pain is not here to destroy you—it's here to reveal you. The question is, Will you let it?

CHAPTER 4

EMPATHY THROUGH ADVERSITY

Pain has a way of reshaping us, whether we want it to or not. It cracks us open, forces us to feel deeply, and leaves us forever changed. We don't come out of suffering the same way we entered it —pain has the power to harden us or soften us, to make us bitter or to make us better. But one of the most profound gifts of pain— though it rarely feels like a gift at the time—is that it makes us more human.

Before we've suffered, it's easy to assume we understand what others are going through. We might offer a kind word, say "I'm sorry for your loss," or tell someone we'll pray for them. And while those gestures are well-meaning, there's a difference between acknowledging someone's pain and feeling it with them.

True empathy—the kind that reaches deep into the soul of another person's suffering and says, "I see you. I feel this with you. You are not alone"—only comes when we've walked through our own darkness.

Pain Changes Your Perspective

When you've experienced real pain, your perspective shifts. Suffering becomes something tangible, a weight that lingers in your body and mind long after the moment has passed. Pain is not just about the event itself—it's about the burden it leaves behind.

You begin to hear it in someone's voice catching mid-sentence, see it in the forced smiles that don't reach their eyes, and recognize it in the way they withdraw from conversations, desperately trying to convince the world they're fine when they're barely holding on. You know it because you've been there. You've felt that weight, too. More importantly, suffering strips away judgment. It's easy to wonder why others aren't handling their pain better when you haven't been broken. But once you've been shattered, you understand that healing isn't linear. Wounds take time, and sometimes, people don't need advice—they need someone willing to sit with them in their pain.

Sympathy vs. Empathy: The Real Difference

Before I experienced my own suffering, I lacked real empathy. I dismissed depression as something only weak people experienced. To me, strength meant pulling yourself together and moving on. I thought pain was something you had to get over.

But then pain found me.

I realized that sometimes, you can't get over it. Sometimes, no matter how much you try to move on, the weight of suffering keeps you in place.

That experience didn't just change me—it humbled me. It forced me to see what I hadn't before: the difference between sympathy and empathy.

Sympathy is acknowledging pain from a distance. Imagine someone stuck in a deep pit. Sympathy stands at the top, looks down, and says, "Wow, that looks awful. I'm so sorry you're down there. I hope you feel better soon." It comes from a place of concern, but it lacks connection. It avoids discomfort.

Empathy, on the other hand, climbs down into the pit with them. Empathy says, "I've been in this darkness. I know what it's like down here. You're not alone. We're going to get through this together." It doesn't try to fix the pain; it chooses to be present in it.

Here's another way to look at it:

- Sympathy sends flowers to someone grieving. Empathy shows up, sits on the couch, and cries with them.
- says, "At least..." Empathy says, "That must be so hard. I can't imagine how heavy this feels."
- Sympathy can sometimes feel dismissive, even when it's well-intentioned. Empathy validates.

The truth about empathy? It requires vulnerability. You can't empathize if you're pretending pain doesn't touch you. Real empathy demands acknowledging your own wounds and using that understanding to meet others where they are.

Pain Inspires Compassion

Once you've been in the darkness yourself, you feel compelled to help others. You recognize pain in others and want to ease it however you can.

Think about addiction counselors who were once addicts themselves. Their ability to relate comes from experience, not training. Or consider the cancer survivor who volunteers at hospitals, providing comfort to patients by saying, "I know how terrifying this feels. And you're not alone."

Pain isolates, but it also connects. It reminds us that we are all human, all fragile, all in need of understanding. And if we let it, pain can soften us, humble us, and make us more capable of love.

How to Use Your Pain to Help Others

Empathy isn't a feeling—it's something you do. It's turning your suffering into something meaningful. Here's how:

Share Your Story: Your transparency could be the lifeline someone else needs to hold on for one more day. For example, consider someone who overcame a traumatic event, like the loss of a loved one, and now runs support groups to help others navigate grief. Their story isn't a recounting of pain; it's a roadmap of hope.

Listen Without Fixing: Sometimes, people don't need solutions. They need someone to say, "I see you. I hear you. I'm with you." For instance, a friend who consistently checks in and listens without judgment can be a powerful force in someone's healing journey.

Be Present in Someone's Pain: Let them talk. Let them cry. Let them be where they are without pushing them to "move on." Therapists, mentors, or caring friends who offer their presence without trying to "fix" someone's pain are invaluable.

Find a Way to Serve: Whether it's mentoring, volunteering, or reaching out to a struggling friend, use your experience to lighten someone else's burden. For example, a recovering addict who becomes a sponsor to others battling addiction, offering both guidance and hope from a place of genuine understanding.

Pain taught you something. Now, let it teach someone else through you. That's the power of empathy born through adversity.

CHAPTER 5

THE MIRROR EFFECT:
PAIN AND SELF-AWARENESS

Pain has a way of demanding our attention. It doesn't wait for the right moment. It doesn't ask for permission. It just shows up—unexpected, disruptive, and unrelenting. It throws our routines into chaos, shakes our sense of security, and forces us to confront the parts of ourselves we've been trying to ignore.

It reveals the wounds we've left untreated, the relationships we know are toxic but refuse to let go of, the habits that comfort us but quietly keep us stuck, and the mindsets that trap us in the same old cycles.

Most of us don't want to face pain. So we try to outrun it. We stay busy with work. We jump from relationship to relationship. We binge shows, scroll endlessly, go out too often—anything that helps us avoid what's really going on inside. And for a while, it works. Until it doesn't.

Because pain has a purpose. And when it shows up, it's not trying to destroy us. It's trying to wake us up.

Pain Is a Mirror That Tells the Truth

Pain is honest. It shows you what you've been pretending not to see. When life is easy, it's easy to avoid the truth. But when pain shows up, it removes the mask. It makes you look at yourself—really look. It forces you to face the lies you've told yourself just to keep going. It shows you where you've settled. It makes you question the coping strategies that no longer serve you. And often, it brings up wounds from the past that you thought were long gone.

Take Jenna, for example. She was a high performer—always working, always pushing forward. She told herself she had moved on from her childhood trauma. She believed staying busy was proof that she was fine. But when she hit burnout, the walls came down. She started having anxiety attacks at work. She felt numb in her relationships. Therapy revealed that her busyness was actually avoidance. Underneath it all was a little girl who never felt safe, who learned to earn love by performing. Until Jenna faced that pain, she couldn't begin to heal.

Then there's Marcus. A top-level executive, respected by many, driven by success. But behind the suits and schedules was a man grieving the breakdown of his marriage. He didn't talk about it. Instead, he buried himself in work. The long hours were his escape. But over time, his health started to suffer. He was constantly sick, exhausted, and angry. One night, after a stress-induced ER visit, Marcus realized he couldn't outrun the pain anymore. With help from therapy, he finally connected the dots: his drive for success wasn't ambition—it was avoidance. His need to stay busy came from the fear that if he stopped, the grief would crush him. That realization was the start of his healing.

Pain doesn't just show us what's wrong. It shows us what needs our attention. If we feel anxious in a relationship that should feel peaceful, that's a red flag. If we numb ourselves with food, substances, or busyness, that's pain trying to speak. If we keep replaying the same hurtful memories, it means something inside of us still hasn't healed.

Pain doesn't lie. It tells the truth we've been avoiding.

Self-Awareness: The Beginning of Real Change

Self-awareness is the first step toward healing. Without it, we stay stuck. We repeat the same behaviors, tell ourselves the same stories, and expect different results. But when we become aware— when we finally see the patterns—we gain power.

We have a choice:
We can continue numbing and pretending.
Or we can lean in, listen, and allow the pain to teach us.

Pain isn't here to punish you. It's here to show you what still needs healing. It's not the enemy. It's the invitation.

Tools for Building Self-Awareness

Awareness doesn't happen by accident. You have to work at it. Here are the tools that helped me—and can help you—turn pain into growth:

- **Therapy: The Deep Dive**

Therapy helps you get below the surface. A skilled therapist will help you trace your pain to its root. You may walk in talking about a recent breakup but end up uncovering abandonment wounds from childhood. That's the power of therapy.

It helped me see how much of my behavior was shaped by unresolved hurt. I didn't just react to today's problems—I was reacting to years of buried pain. Once I saw that, I could start making changes that lasted.

Try This: If you're in therapy or considering it, start by bringing one moment that triggered a strong emotion. Ask yourself—and your therapist—Where is this really coming from?

- **Self-Reflection: Your Personal Insight Tool**

Journaling changed everything for me. When I wrote things down, I began to see patterns I hadn't noticed before. I started asking deeper questions:

1. Why does this bother me so much?
2. Is this reaction about today, or is it tied to something from my past?

3.What belief do I have about myself that might be fueling this pain?

I stopped reacting out of habit and started responding with intention.

Try This: Every night, write down one moment from your day that triggered a strong emotional reaction. Don't judge it—just explore it. Over time, you'll uncover connections you never noticed before.

- **Honest Conversations With Safe People**

You don't need everyone to understand you—but you do need someone.

The turning point for me was when I could say, "I'm hurting and I don't know what to do," and be met with presence instead of advice. That kind of listening is healing. It helps you feel seen when you can't see yourself clearly.

Find the people who can sit in your pain without rushing to fix it. And if you don't have those people yet—start by being that person for yourself.

Awareness, Then Acceptance

As Nathaniel Branden (author of the Power of Esteem) once said: "The first step toward change is awareness. The second step is acceptance."

It's one thing to know where your pain is coming from. It's another to accept what it's showing you and decide to grow from it.

You may need to let go of relationships that feel familiar but unhealthy. You may need to break habits that numb instead of heal. You may need to challenge beliefs you've carried for years—beliefs about your worth, your identity, and your potential.

All of that takes courage. But on the other side of that courage is freedom.

Final Thoughts

Pain is a mirror. It reflects back what we need to heal. But growth doesn't come from looking—it comes from doing something with what we see.

So here's your challenge:

Stop picking up the magnifying glass to examine everyone else.
Pick up the mirror. Look at yourself. Not with shame—but with honesty. And then decide: What do I want to do differently now that I see clearly?

When you do that, pain stops feeling like punishment—and starts becoming your greatest teacher.
So don't waste it.
Let it reveal you.
Let it refine you.
And let it lead you into the version of yourself that's been waiting on the other side of your healing.

CHAPTER 6

FINDING JOY IN THE CONTRASTS

My old pastor's administrative assistant, Daryl Randolph, once said something I'll never forget:

"Everyone in this room is either in a storm, coming out of a storm, or headed into a storm."

At first, I nodded in quiet agreement. That's true for a lot of people, I thought. But over time, I realized it's true for all of us. Storms are part of life. They don't ask permission. They arrive unannounced, shake our routines, and leave us trying to make sense of what's left.
But if storms are inevitable, so is the stillness between them. That's what we forget. The calm is also real—and just as sacred.
We may not get to choose when the storms come, but we do get to choose how we show up when the skies are clear.

Pain Makes Joy Visible

Pain teaches us what peace really means. It sharpens our vision. It forces us to notice things we used to overlook: a quiet morning, a deep belly laugh, a simple walk with someone you love.

Have you ever taken those things for granted?

Most of us have. When life is steady, we slip into autopilot. We rush through our days without noticing the joy we're living in.
But once you've been shaken by pain—whether it's loss, heartbreak, illness, or failure—you begin to see differently. You no longer assume joy is automatic. You realize it's fragile. And you treasure it more.

- After illness, walking without pain feels like a gift.
- After a breakup, genuine connection feels rare and sacred.
- After grief, a simple conversation with someone you love can feel like a miracle.

It's only after being in the dark that we truly appreciate the light.

Faith on the Journey

I'm a believer in Jesus. I trust in God, and I hold on to scriptures like "The joy of the Lord is my strength" (Nehemiah 8:10) and "Peace that surpasses all understanding." (Philippians 4:7). I've experienced those promises in real life. But I've also sat in church with a numb heart. I've prayed through tears and still felt alone.

Here's what I've learned: Faith doesn't make you immune to pain. Even the most devoted people have their low moments. Even the strongest prayers sometimes feel like they go unanswered.

But faith reminds you that peace will come again. It teaches you to wait well. To trust that joy isn't gone forever—it's just buried beneath the weight of what you're walking through.

Faith Looks Different for Everyone

For some, faith is rooted in church, prayer, and scripture. For others, it's found in hope, in the belief that something greater is guiding them, in the strength of family or community. Faith might look like a quiet belief that tomorrow can be better, or like a daily commitment to show up despite the odds.

Whatever your version looks like, the message is the same:

Don't overlook joy just because life is calm. Don't assume peace will always be there.
Joy is a gift—not a guarantee.

Lena's Story: Rediscovering Joy

Lena used to start her days slow and intentional. She'd sip coffee on the porch and watch the sunrise, letting the silence anchor her. But as life picked up pace, that routine slipped away. Work calls replaced quiet mornings. Emails came before breakfast. And without realizing it, she stopped noticing the sky altogether.
Then came the storm.

A sudden and devastating loss knocked the air out of her lungs. The silence she once cherished now felt heavy. The sunrise still came, but she never looked up.
Weeks passed. One morning, restless and weary, she stepped outside just to breathe.

And there it was—the sky painted in gold and lavender. The same sunrise that had always been there. This time, it stopped her.
Tears welled in her eyes. Not just from sadness, but from the realization: She had forgotten how to notice the beauty she once lived for.

That morning marked a shift. Lena didn't magically heal overnight. But she made a promise—to never let joy slip by unnoticed again.

When Joy Returns... So Does Guilt

When I started feeling joy again—when I laughed without forcing it or had a peaceful day without chaos—I felt something unexpected: guilt.

- How can I enjoy this when I've hurt people?
- After all the damage I caused, do I even deserve peace?
- What if I let my guard down and it all falls apart again?

I didn't feel worthy of joy. I felt like I had to earn it. Maybe you've felt that way too.

But here's the truth: **Joy isn't earned. It's allowed.**

It's not a reward for perfect behavior. It's a part of healing. It's a reminder that even broken people can laugh again, love again, and live again.

Gratitude in the Middle of the Storm

Gratitude is a skill. One that requires practice—especially when life feels like it's falling apart.

Gratitude doesn't ignore pain. It acknowledges it while still choosing to see what's good.
- A moment of laughter in a hard day.
- A friend checking in unexpectedly.
- The ability to get out of bed when yesterday, you couldn't.

Gratitude doesn't mean your life is perfect. It means you've decided not to let pain erase everything beautiful in your world.

Joy Is Not the End Goal—It's the Strength Along the Way

So many of us think we'll feel joy after the storm passes. But joy is not just the reward at the end of suffering. It's what helps us survive it.

Joy is not the absence of pain—it's the quiet strength that helps us keep going despite it.
It's the cup of coffee in the middle of a hard day. It's the smile that surprises you through tears. It's the reminder that life still holds good things, even when you're holding grief.

Ask Yourself: What Have I Been Missing?

Right now, take a moment and ask:
- What have I stopped noticing?
- What brings me peace that I've been overlooking?
- Where is joy showing up, quietly, waiting to be seen?

Because the truth is: **Joy is still here. Peace is still possible. But you have to open your eyes to see it.**

Let your pain teach you. But let your joy carry you.
Don't wait for a perfect life to be thankful. **Let this moment be enough.**

Because when you stop taking joy for granted, you start living with your eyes wide open—and that kind of living changes everything.

CHAPTER 7

THE ART OF PATIENCE AND ACCEPTANCE

One of the greatest lessons pain has ever taught me is how to be patient—with myself and with the process of healing.

If you've ever been in deep pain, you know what I mean. You've probably begged for the storm to pass, for the heartache to lift, for the grief to finally let you breathe. I've been there. But I learned the hard way: healing can't be rushed. The more you try to speed through it, the more likely you are to find yourself facing the same pain again—because you never allowed yourself to fully heal the first time.

We live in a culture that glorifies instant results—fast food, two-day shipping, instant downloads. But healing doesn't work like that. Especially emotional healing. A broken leg has a timeline. A broken heart doesn't.

There's no set calendar for mending a shattered sense of self-worth or recovering from deep betrayal. That uncertainty is what makes patience so hard. But it's also what makes it necessary.

Healing Takes Trust

What I've realized is this: most of us don't struggle with patience because we're naturally impatient. We struggle because we don't trust the process. We try to force healing because we're afraid it won't happen otherwise. We want to control the timeline so we don't feel helpless. But healing isn't something you control — t's something you allow.

And that takes trust.

This became crystal clear in a case where a patient living with persistent psychosis found little relief in traditional therapy. He was overwhelmed by delusions and paranoia, and his instinct, like so many of us, was to fight the pain. But through Acceptance and Commitment Therapy (ACT), he learned to accept his thoughts without judgment—to stop resisting and start acknowledging. Over time, his distress lessened, and his ability to function improved. It wasn't that the pain disappeared—it was that his relationship with it changed. That's the power of trust.

The Difference Between Patience and Passivity

A common misunderstanding is confusing patience with passivity. But they aren't the same.

Patience is active. It means doing the emotional work, staying present in the discomfort, and trusting that progress is happening, even if it's not visible yet.

Passivity is avoidance. It's distracting yourself, suppressing emotions, or numbing out and hoping time alone will do the healing for you.

Many people believe they're being patient when they're really just avoiding. Time, by itself, doesn't heal. It's what you do with that time that creates healing.

Real-Life Examples: Elijah and Renee

Take Elijah, for example. After a painful breakup, he dove into work and weekend distractions. From the outside, he looked like he was "moving on." But inside, he was stuck—avoiding, not healing.

Then there's Renee, who faced her pain directly. She gave herself space to feel. She journaled, attended therapy, and let herself cry. She wasn't just passing time—she was participating in her healing. That's the difference.

Healing Through Creativity and Expression

Some people can't articulate their pain with words—and that's okay. In another powerful case, a woman who had buried years of trauma found her breakthrough through art therapy. When words failed her, painting gave her a voice. With each brushstroke, she externalized pain she couldn't say out loud. Through color and canvas, she processed trauma and reclaimed power over her story. That too is healing. That too is patience.

Whether it's a paintbrush or a prayer, your healing doesn't have to look like anyone else's. But it does have to be honest.

When You Rush the Process, You Restart the Pain

Think of an athlete recovering from a broken collarbone. The doctor says, "You're healing well, but don't play for eight weeks." At week five, he feels great—so he plays. Then, in the third quarter, one wrong move and snap—he's back to square one. Not because he wasn't healing, but because he didn't trust the timeline.

We do this emotionally all the time. We rush into new relationships or responsibilities before we've processed the last loss. Then we wonder why we keep ending up in the same pain. Healing takes time—and trust.

Acceptance: Letting Go of Control

The hardest part of healing is acceptance—not of what happened, but of the fact that we can't change it. We hold onto the past like a lifeline. We replay what we should've done, how it could've gone. We think, If I just had another chance...

But peace begins where resistance ends.
Acceptance isn't passive. It's powerful. It says, This hurt me. I didn't choose it. But I won't let it define me forever.

The Power of Story: Healing Through Others' Journeys

Sometimes, it helps just to know we're not alone. In a recent study, individuals experiencing depression and anxiety were asked to listen to real stories of recovery. The impact was profound. Just hearing others say, "I've been there, and I made it through" gave them hope—and made healing feel possible.

That's what your story can do for someone else. That's what someone else's story might be doing for you, even right now.

How to Practice Patience and Acceptance

Here are four tools that have helped me slow down, trust the process, and stop resisting what I couldn't change:

- **Mindfulness and Meditation**

Learn to sit with your emotions without judgment. Meditation teaches you to witness, not react. When you stop fighting pain, you give it space to pass.

- **Focus on Small Steps**

Instead of asking, "When will I be healed?" ask, "What's one good thing I can do for myself today?" One walk. One deep breath. One honest journal entry. That's progress.

- **Reframe Setbacks**

A hard day doesn't mean you're failing. It means you're healing. And healing isn't linear. Expect the waves—but trust that they're carrying you somewhere.

- **Let Go of Timelines**

Stop comparing your healing to someone else's highlight reel. Your process isn't late. It's on time.

Final Thoughts

Patience and acceptance are two of the hardest things pain asks of us. They require trust. They require stillness. And they require us to give up our timelines.

But they are also the foundation for real, lasting healing.
They help you stop reopening wounds. They allow you to breathe again. They give you permission to be human.

So if you're in the middle of the storm—don't rush it. Don't try to numb it. Don't waste it. Let it teach you. Let it transform you. Because healing isn't just about getting back to who you were—it's about discovering who you're becoming.

CHAPTER 8

BOUNDARIES BORN FROM PAIN

Pain is a ruthless teacher. It doesn't hand out lessons gently—it slams them down in front of us. It forces us to confront uncomfortable truths, shines a light on where we've let things slide too long, and demands that we take a stand for ourselves. One of the hardest—but most necessary—lessons pain teaches us is the importance of boundaries.

Pain reveals where boundaries should have existed, where they were ignored, and where they now must be built. It exposes the moments when we've been too lenient with others and far too harsh with ourselves. It brings to light the relationships where we've given too much, the jobs that have drained us, the expectations that have exhausted us.

Sometimes, the deepest pain doesn't come from what someone did to us—but from the gut-wrenching realization that we allowed it.
I say that not to shame you, but to share a truth I wish I'd accepted sooner: where there are no boundaries, pain will follow.

The Cost of No Boundaries

For a long time, I was a people pleaser. I hated saying no. I didn't want to let anyone down, even if that meant constantly letting myself down in the process. It didn't matter how inconvenient, costly, or emotionally draining it was—I said yes.
Why? Because I wanted to be the dependable one. The strong one. The "go-to" person.

But underneath that smile was a silent scream. Because behind the image I was trying to uphold, I had no boundaries.

I did things I didn't want to do. I stayed in relationships that chipped away at my self-worth. I tolerated disrespect in the name of keeping the peace. And in the end? I wasn't at peace at all.
I was exhausted—physically, emotionally, and spiritually.

People had come to expect my constant availability, and I had taught them to. I had taught them that I didn't require limits. That my needs came last. And the scariest part? I didn't even realize it until I hit a wall of burnout so hard that it made me question who I really was.

Pain as a Warning Sign

Pain isn't always loud. It doesn't always show up like a crashing wave. Sometimes, it starts as a whisper:
- The pit in your stomach when someone asks for one more favor and you say yes, even though you're stretched thin.
- The frustration after a conversation that leaves you drained because you gave too much and got nothing in return.
- The heaviness after spending hours fixing someone else's crisis, while your own needs sit unattended.

I remember feeling irritable all the time but not knowing why. I blamed stress. I blamed work. But really, I was mad at myself—for never saying no. For always being available. For letting my boundaries erode until there was nothing left to protect.

Pain was my warning sign. It was saying: You're giving away pieces of yourself you were never meant to lose.

What Crossed Boundaries Can Look Like

Let's talk about this in a way that feels real. Maybe you've lived these moments too:

You say yes, even though your heart is screaming no.
You commit to helping someone move, host an event, or take on

another work project—even though you're mentally and physically depleted. You smile through it, but inside, there's resentment growing.

You feel obligated to fix everyone's problems.
Someone unloads their emotional weight on you again, and instead of offering support, you feel responsible. You cancel your plans to talk them through it—for the fifth time this week.

You replay conversations in your head, wondering if you were too harsh for setting a limit.
You finally speak up and say, "I can't do that for you right now." And even though it was the right thing to do, you spend the rest of the night battling guilt.

These are all signs of overstepped boundaries. And the pain that follows isn't random—it's your soul's way of saying: This isn't sustainable.

Selfishness vs. Self-Preservation

Let me be clear: setting boundaries is not selfish. We've been conditioned to believe that protecting our peace makes us cold or uncaring. That saying no means we don't love people.

But that's not true.

Selfishness is taking more than you give without concern for others. Self-preservation is giving without losing yourself in the process.
The people who benefited from your lack of boundaries may call you selfish once you start saying no. They may accuse you of being distant, unkind, or changing. That's okay. Their discomfort isn't your responsibility. Your healing is.

How to Set Boundaries When You Never Have Before

If you've gone your whole life without boundaries, it won't feel natural at first. But it's necessary. And it's possible.

Let me walk you through how to start:

- **Identify Where Boundaries Are Needed**

Pay attention to where you feel resentment, fatigue, or dread. Those feelings are messengers. If every phone call from a certain person drains you, that's not a coincidence—it's a cue.

- **Define Your Limits**

Get honest about what you can and can't give. What behaviors are you no longer willing to tolerate? What expectations are you no longer going to carry?

- **Start Small**

You don't have to set a boundary by burning bridges. Try saying, "I can't make it tonight," or "I need some time to myself." Boundaries build over time. Confidence grows with each one you set.

- **Communicate Without Apology**

You don't need to justify why you're setting a boundary. You're not being rude. You're being real. "No" is a complete sentence.

- **Expect Resistance**

People may push back. They may test you. That doesn't mean your boundary is wrong. It means it's working.

- **Enforce Boundaries with Action**

If someone consistently ignores your limits, don't keep repeating them. Enforce them. Step back. Redirect your energy. Protect your peace.

- **Release the Guilt**

The people who truly love you will adjust. The ones who don't? They were never invested in the real you—only in what they could take from you.

Why Boundaries Matter

Pain will show you exactly where the boundary should've been. You'll feel it when you're overextending. You'll hear it in your own silence when your needs go unspoken. You'll sense it in your body—

tight shoulders, racing thoughts, exhaustion—for what you keep tolerating.

But when you set a boundary, you choose you.

You stop bleeding for people who wouldn't offer you a Band-Aid.
You stop performing for approval that never comes.
You stop waiting for permission to protect your peace.

Final Thoughts

Boundaries aren't about shutting people out.
They're about **keeping yourself whole**.
You are not here to be everything to everyone.
You are here to live with intention, to love without losing yourself.

Pain may have exposed the cracks in your life—but boundaries are how you rebuild. Stronger. Wiser. Healthier.

So start today. Draw the line. Hold it with kindness. And don't let guilt talk you out of protecting the peace you fought so hard to find. Your worth doesn't require exhaustion to be proven.

Let pain teach you. Let boundaries heal you.
And above all—don't waste what you've learned.

CHAPTER 9

THE TEMPORARY NATURE OF SUFFERING (AND HAPPINESS)

Pain teaches us something we all need to remember: nothing—good or bad—lasts forever.

When we're in the middle of suffering, it can feel endless. The discomfort stretches across our days and into our nights, making hope feel far away. But just like the seasons change and tides rise and fall, our hardships eventually shift. No matter how overwhelming it feels, this moment is just that—a moment. And moments pass.

Both pain and happiness are temporary. They ebb and flow, often without warning. One minute you're at peace, the next you're reeling. A single phone call can change everything. But instead of asking, How long will this last? try asking, What is this here to teach me?

When we stop resisting pain and start learning from it, we begin to grow. And just as happiness eventually returns, so does healing.

All Emotions Are Temporary: Pain Will Pass—But So Will Happiness

No emotion lasts forever. Whether it's grief, anger, happiness, or contentment—each has its own season. Pain may feel like it's stretching endlessly, like it's dug its roots into your soul. But over time, it loosens its grip.

And happiness? Happiness is just as fleeting. Those moments of deep connection, laughter, celebration—they may be brief, but they are precious.

Knowing this doesn't make pain easier, but it helps us hold happiness with open hands. We stop trying to bottle it up or make it last forever. We learn to experience it fully while it's here. And when it leaves, we don't panic—we remember that it will come back.

The same principle helps us endure pain. We stop letting it define us, and we start letting it pass through us. We feel it, but we know it won't stay forever.

The One Thing That Lasts: True Love

Amid the emotional highs and lows, one thing has staying power: love.

Not just romantic love or fleeting affection, but real love—the kind grounded in choice and commitment. The kind of love that stays when feelings fade, that continues showing up when things are hard.

Whether it's the love we receive from others or the love we learn to give ourselves, this kind of love is our anchor. It weathers storms. It survives seasons. It reminds us who we are when life feels uncertain.

When everything else changes, love is what remains.

Why Embracing Impermanence Makes You Stronger
Impermanence can feel unsettling because we crave certainty. But once we accept that nothing in life stays the same, we begin to find strength in that truth.

It means that no matter how painful this season is, it will pass.It means that no success or failure defines us forever.It means we don't have to cling to what was or fear what's to come.

Embracing impermanence frees us to live in the now. It gives us permission to grow, adapt, and keep moving forward.

Two Different Responses to Change

Let's take a look at two people—Maya and Daniel—who faced unexpected change. Their reactions reveal just how much our perspective shapes our healing.

Maya: Embracing Change

Maya is a freelance designer who suddenly lost her biggest client—the contract that paid most of her bills. At first, she panicked. Doubts crept in. What if I can't find another opportunity? What if I fail?

But instead of spiraling, Maya gave herself space to grieve the loss. She didn't deny her fear, but she didn't let it define her either. She started waking up early again, something she hadn't done in years. She used the time to sketch, journal, and explore an idea she had been sitting on for months—a line of hand-drawn prints she had always wanted to launch.

It wasn't easy. There were setbacks and slow weeks. But over time, Maya's side passion turned into a small business. Not only did she replace her lost income, but she also rediscovered parts of herself that had been buried in the hustle.

Maya didn't bounce back—she bounced forward. By embracing impermanence, she used the loss as a doorway to something new. Her willingness to surrender to the season she was in became the foundation of her resilience.

Daniel: Fighting Change

Daniel's story is the opposite. When his long-term relationship ended, he couldn't accept it. He played every conversation in his head, obsessed over what went wrong, and convinced himself he would never love again.

Instead of healing, Daniel held onto the pain. He avoided new friendships, turned down opportunities, and spent his energy trying to fix the past. While time passed, he didn't move forward. He remained emotionally stuck, because he couldn't accept that the chapter had closed.

Daniel's pain wasn't deeper than Maya's—but his resistance to change made his suffering linger.

Their stories highlight this truth: pain is inevitable, but suffering is often a result of resistance. When we stop fighting the season we're in, we create room for healing.

Peace Doesn't Come From a Perfect Life

We think peace means no problems, but real peace is something deeper. It's not about avoiding pain it's about knowing you can survive it. It's about feeling sadness and still trusting that joy will return. It's about having chaos around you, but calm within you.
This kind of peace isn't passive—it's practiced.

Final Thoughts: Nothing Lasts Forever–But Peace Can Stay With You

Whatever season you're in—whether joy or sorrow—remember this: it's temporary. The highs and the lows will both fade. But peace? Peace can stay, even when everything else shifts.
So breathe deeply.Stay present.Let the storm pass—without becoming the storm.
Because in every season, peace is still possible.
And if you hold on to that, you won't just survive—you'll grow.

CHAPTER 10

THE FREEDOM TO FEEL WITHOUT SUFFERING

The Truth About Feeling vs. Suffering

We're often taught to believe that pain and suffering are the same. That if we hurt, we must also struggle. But that isn't true. Pain is a part of life—suffering is what we add to it.

Pain is what happens. Suffering is the story we attach to it: "Why me?" or "I'll never be okay again." For example, losing a loved one is painful. That grief is natural. But suffering is when we live in a cycle of regret, reliving every moment and never allowing ourselves to move forward.

We don't have to fear our feelings. We have to feel them. Fully. Without shame, without judgment, and without attaching them to our worth.

Reflection Prompt:
Think of a painful moment in your life. What was the story you attached to it? How much of your suffering came from the event—and how much from your interpretation of it?

The Illusion of Control

We try to control our emotions by suppressing them. We smile when we're breaking. We distract ourselves, hoping that if we ignore our feelings long enough, they'll disappear. But what we resist only grows stronger.

True strength isn't found in avoidance—it's found in the courage to feel.

Reflection Prompt:
What emotions have you been avoiding lately? Why?
What would it look like to allow yourself to feel them, even briefly?

Daniel's Crossroads: Suffering or Surrender

Meet Daniel.

He had spent nearly a decade building his dream career. Late nights, missed holidays, personal sacrifices—he poured everything into his job because it made him feel seen, valued, and in control. But all of that changed with one unexpected meeting and a short conversation that ended with: "We're letting you go."

In a matter of minutes, Daniel's identity unraveled. His first reaction wasn't sadness—it was shock, then anger, then shame. The voices in his head grew louder: How could this happen? What did I do wrong? Who am I without this job?

At first, he chose the path many of us choose when we're blindsided by pain: he isolated himself. He stopped answering texts. He turned down every invitation to connect. Nights were filled with restless scrolling and one too many drinks. "I just need time," he told himself. But the truth was, he wasn't giving himself time to heal—he was trying to avoid the fact that he was broken.

The spiral continued for weeks. He couldn't bring himself to update his résumé or even glance at job postings. He felt like a failure, and worse, he believed it. He convinced himself no one would understand how much this loss had affected him—not just financially, but emotionally, spiritually.

Until one night, after finishing another bottle of whiskey and staring at the ceiling in the dark, Daniel finally said aloud: "I can't keep doing this."

That was his turning point.

The next morning, he called his sister—a therapist—and told her everything. For the first time, he spoke the truth without hiding behind pride. She didn't interrupt. She didn't rush him. She just listened. And when he was done, she gently asked, "Are you ready to stop fighting yourself and start feeling again?"

Something clicked.

Over the next few weeks, Daniel did what once felt impossible—he surrendered. Not to the pain, but to the process of healing. He booked his first therapy appointment. He started journaling in the mornings, pouring out the thoughts that had been suffocating him for months. He began walking daily, just to clear his head. Some days he cried during those walks. Some days he felt numb. But every day, he kept showing up.

He also reconnected with his support system—friends he had pushed away, mentors he hadn't spoken to in years. One friend, who had also gone through a major career change,became a steady reminder that life after loss wasn't only possible—it could be purposeful.

One evening, during a therapy session, his counselor said, "You didn't just lose a job, Daniel. You lost a version of yourself you believed you had to be in order to be worthy."

That sentence wrecked him. But it also released him.

He realized he had tied his self-worth to productivity, to validation from others, to achievements. Losing his job forced him to meet himself without the title, without the paycheck, without the applause—and discover he was still enough.

Over time, Daniel didn't just recover—he redefined who he was. One evening, during a therapy session, his counselor said, "You didn't just lose a job, Daniel. You lost a version of yourself you believed you had to be in order to be worthy."

That sentence wrecked him. But it also released him.

He realized he had tied his self-worth to productivity, to validation from others, to achievements. Losing his job forced him to meet himself without the title, without the paycheck, without the applause—and discover he was still enough.

Over time, Daniel didn't just recover—he redefined who he was.

He didn't bounce back to the same life. He bounced forward into something new. He took a consulting role, one that gave him flexibility and time to work on a passion project he had shelved years ago. More importantly, he learned to check in with his emotions regularly, to honor his inner world rather than hide from it.

Reflection Prompt:
Think about a time you experienced loss, disappointment, or failure.
Did you lean into the pain—or try to outrun it?
What could surrender have looked like in that moment?

The Weight of Emotional Resistance
We don't realize how much energy we waste avoiding our emotions. The sadness we distract ourselves from. The anger we bury. The grief we pretend isn't there.

Unfelt emotions don't leave. They settle in our bodies—showing up as anxiety, exhaustion, even physical illness.

The more we resist, the more power our emotions gain.

Quick Exercise:
Close your eyes. Take three deep breaths.
Ask yourself: What feeling is sitting just below the surface right now?
Name it. That's your first step to releasing it.

How to Feel Without Being Consumed

Feeling deeply doesn't mean drowning in emotions. It means giving them permission to move through you.

- Emotions are visitors. Let them in. Let them go.
- Name the feeling without becoming it. Say, "I feel sadness," not "I am sad."
- Stop judging what you feel. Emotions aren't good or bad—they just are.

Reflection Prompt:

What emotion do you often judge or shame yourself for feeling? What might change if you gave yourself permission to feel it fully?

What Your Emotions Are Trying to Tell You

Every emotion carries a message:

- **Sadness** shows us what we love.
- **Anger** reveals what we value.
- **Fear** highlights where courage is needed.
- **Guilt** invites us to return to our values.

Ask yourself: What is this emotion trying to show me?

Mini Journaling Prompt:
Pick one emotion you've felt this week.
What triggered it? What might it be pointing you toward?
Healthy Ways to Move Emotion

Let your emotions move through you—not stay stuck inside. Here are tools that help:

- Journaling: Write without censoring.
- Talking: Call a friend who will truly listen.
- Movement: Walk, stretch, dance—just move.
- Creativity: Paint, draw, make music.
- Stillness: Sit. Breathe. Let yourself feel.

Try This Now:

Set a timer for 5 minutes. Write down everything you feel—no editing, no judgment.

When the timer ends, ask: What did I learn from that emotion?

The Real Meaning of Peace

Peace doesn't mean you stop feeling. It means your emotions don't control you. You can be calm even in chaos. You can hold sadness and still feel grounded.

Peace isn't the absence of emotion. It's the ability to experience emotion without fear.

Reflection Prompt:
What would peace look like in your life right now—not perfection, but peace?

Final Thoughts: Let the Storm Pass Without Becoming the Storm

What if you stopped running from your emotions? What if you made room for all of them—without fear, without guilt, without shame?

This is emotional freedom: feeling fully without being consumed.

Let the storm come. Let it move through you. Trust that it will pass. You don't have to become your pain to feel it. You don't have to suffer to heal.

You just have to feel.

Final Reflection:
What emotions are you ready to stop fighting?
What kind of peace do you believe is possible on the other side of that surrender?

CHAPTER 11

HOW TO HEAL WITHOUT WASTING THE PAIN

Throughout this book, I've shared practical steps to help navigate pain and view it through a different lens. But now, let's take a deeper dive into what it truly means to heal without wasting your pain. Because healing isn't just about surviving—it's about growing wiser, stronger, and more connected to yourself through the process.

The Misconceptions of Emotional Healing

Many believe healing is a straight path—each step bringing you closer to a moment when the pain is gone. But healing doesn't work like that. It's not a destination. It's an ongoing journey filled with progress, setbacks, and personal revelations.

People often think if they're still triggered by past events, they haven't truly healed. But healing doesn't erase memory or prevent emotion—it changes how we respond. Triggers don't mean failure; they reveal where healing still needs attention.

Another misconception is that healing happens with time alone. While time may soften pain, it doesn't resolve it. Avoidance and silence allow pain to linger, influencing how we think, act, and relate to others.

Many also believe healing should be done in isolation—that real strength means doing it alone. But more often, healing comes through connection—whether in therapy, meaningful conversation, or being truly heard.

Lastly, healing is sometimes misinterpreted as being happy all the time. But healing isn't about avoiding negative emotions. It's about learning how to sit with them, honor them, and understand what they're teaching you.

Healing Is Personal—There's No One-Size-Fits-All Approach

Self-help culture often promotes a universal formula for healing. But what works for one person might not work for another—and that's okay.

When I started therapy, it transformed my life. I became an advocate, believing everyone should go. But I eventually realized not everyone heals the same way. Some people need creative outlets. Others find peace through movement, solitude, or faith. Healing is deeply personal, and it evolves as we grow.

Just because one path doesn't work doesn't mean you're broken. It means you're still learning what works for you.

Reflection Prompt:
What has genuinely helped you feel more whole during difficult seasons? What didn't?

Are You Wasting Your Pain or Using It for Growth?

Pain can break you down—or build you up. But it only becomes wisdom if you face it with intention. Ask yourself:

- **Have I grown from this experience?** Have your boundaries changed? Have your priorities shifted?

- **Have I truly forgiven?** Not excused—but released the emotional grip someone or something had over you?

- **Am I still replaying painful memories?** Or am I beginning to see them with new perspective?

- **Am I using pain as a reason to stay stuck?** Or am I choosing to move forward, even if it's slow?

- Have I found meaning in what happened? Even if it still hurts—what has it revealed about your strength, your values, or your purpose?

Real-Life Examples of Growth Through Pain

John's Story

John was deeply betrayed by a friend. He held onto resentment for years, believing forgiveness would let the person off the hook. But over time, he realized that forgiveness wasn't about the other person—it was about his freedom. When he let go of the grudge, he found peace he didn't know he was missing. That choice didn't excuse the betrayal—it broke its control over him.

Forgiveness Tip:

Write a letter to the person who hurt you. You don't have to send it. Just write it. Then write one to yourself. Release what needs to be released.

Emily's Story

Emily lost her job during a recession. At first, the loss crushed her confidence. But instead of staying stuck, she asked, What can I do with this? That question led her to start a nonprofit helping others navigate unemployment. What once felt like the end of everything became the beginning of something meaningful.

Reflection Prompt:

What has your pain revealed to you? What new path might it be inviting you to explore?

Tracking and Celebrating Your Progress

Healing isn't always about dramatic transformation. Sometimes, it's quiet. It's subtle.

It's the way you pause before reacting.It's how you no longer carry the same shame.It's the moment you choose rest instead of guilt. Journaling helps you see these shifts. Over time, you'll notice that t the version of you showing up today is stronger than the one from yesterday.

Exercise: Start a Progress Journal
Each week, write down:

One emotion you allowed yourself to feel
One kind thing you did for yourself
One way you responded differently than before

Healing Is a Daily Choice

Healing without wasting your pain means choosing to grow from what you've been through—not letting it keep you trapped.

It's deciding to look inward with honesty. To forgive yourself. To let go of blame. To trust that even your brokenness can become a blueprint for something beautiful.

You don't need to rush. You don't need to be perfect. You just need to show up—and try.

Final Words

If you take anything away from this chapter, let it be this:
Your healing matters—even when no one sees it.

Your growth might be slow. It might be messy. But it is sacred.

You don't need anyone's timeline. You don't need to be completely over it to be moving forward. You don't need to be healed to begin healing.

So keep going. Keep choosing you. Keep listening to what your pain is trying to teach you.

Because when you refuse to waste it—your pain becomes the very thing that prepares you for the purpose ahead.

CHAPTER 12

WHAT COMES NEXT: LIVING A LIFE TRANSFORMED BY PAIN

At the end of the day, most people don't intentionally waste their pain. Not because they want to—but because they don't realize they're doing it. Pain becomes part of their identity, influencing decisions, behaviors, and beliefs in quiet, unnoticed ways. It seeps into their mindset and echoes in phrases like, "This is just the way I am."

But what if that's not who you really are?

What if who you are now is simply a version of you shaped by survival—not intention?

Who Were You Before the Hurt?

Pause for a moment and think about it.

Were you once more open, more fearless, more hopeful?

Did you chase dreams without second-guessing yourself?

Did you love without hesitation?

Pain changes us. That's inevitable. But healing is how we choose to change back—or change forward. It's the process of reclaiming the parts of ourselves that were lost, buried, or broken in the chaos.

Healing Isn't Erasing the Past—It's Learning From It

Healing doesn't mean forgetting. It means remembering with wisdom, integrating the lessons, and choosing how you want to move forward. Imagine a painter who once filled canvases with bold colors and big ideas. After a deep loss, they put the brush down, convinced their creativity had died with their joy. But healing didn't mean pretending the loss never happened—it meant learning to paint through the pain, letting every shade tell the truth of their story.

Declare the Truth About Who You Are

Say it out loud—even if your voice shakes.
I am not my pain.
I am not what happened to me.
I am not my past, my trauma, or the opinions of others.
I am still here. And I am still becoming.

If you're reading this, it means you've already survived more than you thought you could. The storm didn't take you out. The weeping came—but so did the morning. Let that be your reminder: You are still standing. That matters.

Don't Mistake Walls for Boundaries

A lot of us think healing means shutting everyone out. We build walls, thinking they'll protect us. But all they do is isolate us from connection, love, and growth.

Walls say, "No one gets in."
Boundaries say, "I get to decide who stays."

The goal is not to become hard—it's to become whole. Remembering what happened allows you to set boundaries, not because you're bitter, but because you're wiser.

Your Pain Is Not the End of the Story

Pain may have influenced your life, but it doesn't get the final word. You are not weak for what you've endured. You are strong because of it.

This is your turning point—the moment you stop seeing yourself as a victim of your past and start becoming the architect of your future.

You've been through the fire. Now it's time to rise from the ashes—not as who you were, but as who you were always meant to become.

From Pain to Purpose

This book is a tool. But tools only work if you use them. I know what it's like to go in circles, re-living the same pain, stuck in survival mode. It wasn't until I started leaning into the pain that everything changed.

I stopped asking, "Why did this happen to me?" and started asking,

"What can I learn from this?"

That shift didn't erase my pain—but it gave it purpose.

You Don't Need to Be Perfect—Just Present

You don't need to have it all figured out. You just need to start showing up for yourself. Healing happens in small moments—in the choice to say no, in the willingness to try again, in the courage to rest when you need to.

You are not meant to shrink. You are not meant to stay broken.

You were made to rise.

Real People. Real Stories. Real Growth.

Take John, who spent years imprisoned by resentment after a betrayal. He thought forgiveness meant excusing the hurt. But when he finally let go—not for the other person, but for himself—he found a freedom he didn't know was possible.

Or Emily, who lost her job during a recession and felt like a failure. But instead of letting the pain define her, she started a nonprofit to help others facing unemployment. What once looked like the end became her beginning.

Healing is never wasted when it's used to lift someone else.

Check In With Yourself

Here are a few questions to reflect on:

What pain am I still holding onto that's shaping my behavior?

- What pain am I still holding onto that's shaping my behavior?
- Have I built walls when I should be setting boundaries?
- What would it look like to take one step forward, even if I'm scared?
- How can I turn my pain into purpose, starting now?

Final Thoughts: What Comes Next Is Up to You

You've read the pages. You've done the inner work. Now comes the hardest part: living it out.

You weren't meant to just survive. You were meant to live. Boldly. Joyfully. On purpose.

Your story matters. Your strength matters. And there's someone out there who needs the version of you that chooses healing over hiding.

I'm rooting for you.
I believe in the person God designed you to be.

And I know your best chapter hasn't even been written yet.

So I leave you with this:

Love God. Love people. And love yourself, too.

Never, waste your pain.

Maurice Elston was born and raised in Kansas City, MO, where his love for writing took root at an early age through music and poetry. In college, a professor recognized his talent, pulling him aside to encourage him to take writing more seriously.

However, life led Maurice down a different path—one that took him into the world of sales. Over the years, he built a successful career, coaching and mentoring aspiring sales professionals, helping them navigate their journeys with confidence and skill.

Yet, despite his achievements in sales, Maurice carried a quiet, unshakable dream—to become a published author. While he initially considered fiction, his personal experiences and deep passion for helping others guided him toward the world of self-help.

Now, Maurice is dedicated to helping others discover their purpose through their pain.